Why Flowers Bloom

Also by Janet Carncross Chandler

Flight of the Wild Goose

Why Flowers Bloom

Janet Carncross Chandler

Papier-Mache Press
Watsonville CA

Copyright © 1993 by Janet Carncross Chandler. Printed in the United States of America. All rights reserved including the right to reproduce this book or portions thereof in any form. For information contact Papier-Mache Press, 135 Aviation Way, #14, Watsonville, CA 95076.

ISBN: 0-918949-37-8 Softcover

ISBN: 0-918949-38-6 Hardcover

Cover art by Janet Carncross Chandler

Cover design by Cynthia Heier

Photo credits: p. 83 and p. 104 Bill Chandler. All other photographs by Janet Carncross Chandler.

Typography by Prism Photographics

Grateful acknowledgment is made to the following publications which first published some of the material in this book:

Vintage, A Magazine for Women, 1988 for "On Staying Out"; *Poet News,* October 1989 for "Listening to DeBussy's *La Mer* While Doing Something Else"; *Poet News,* March 1990 for "City"; *KXPR/KXJZ Program Guide,* May 1991 for "Nouveau Peacock"; *KXPR/KXJZ Program Guide,* May 1992 for "I Sing of My Body Eclectic"; *Unitarian Universalist Society of Sacramento,* December 1991 for "Prayer by a Naïf"; *Morality Exchange,* July 1992 for "Death in the Family"; and *Haight Ashbury Literary Journal,* Vol. 6, No. 2, August 1992 for "Dancing at the Senior Center."

Library of Congress Cataloging-in-Publication Data

Chandler, Janet Carncross, 1910-
    Why flowers bloom / Janet Carncross Chandler.
        p.   cm.
    ISBN 0-918949-38-6 (alk. paper) : $12.00—ISBN 0-918949-37-8
(pbk. : alk. paper) : $8.00
    1. Aging—Poetry.   2. Aged women—Poetry.   I. Title.
PS3553.H27123W49   1993
811'.54—dc20   93-39967
                                                                              CIP

To my husband, Bill
our sons, David and Dan
and their families
to old and new friends
and to the many poets and teachers
who influenced my poetic growth

Contents

Why Flowers Bloom

I Sing of My Body Eclectic

(Happy Birthday to Walt Whitman and to me on my eightieth)

I sing of my aging body
two legs lagging at times
more often still striding.

Sometimes I sing of my unwrinkled back
never of my intricately patterned front
always of my face when it smiles.

And I sing of my rheumy eyes
sharper by far with the peeling
of yellowish opaque blinders.

I do sing of my love of color
blues and greens and my new loves—
green-yellow and violet and purple.

I sing too of my good left ear
but not of my right ear's deafness
nor the telltale way I cock my head.

Of course I sing of Bach and Brahms
of Bartok, Beethoven's Ninth, and Ravel.
Moreover, I sing loudly of most jazz.

I sing of religious tolerance
of a church sometimes
more like a walk in a deep wood.

Lustily I sing of broccoli and bananas
and for six trusty vitamins
keeping me from needing medicine.

I often sing praises of my faithful doctors.
Naturally, I sing of social security, medicare
and my Supplementary Health and Dental Insurers.

I surely do sing of that safety thing
on my door, of grab-holds on my bathtub
and emergency pulls I've not yet needed.

I sing of the safety of poet-friends
most of all, of my two sons and their wives.
How I sing of grandson William, granddaughter Sasha.

I hum happily of my body eclectic
sparking still after so many years.
I do *not* sing of loss   aloneness   or death.

Transparencies

As I grow older
it seems to me other people
know better what is in store for me
than I do. It's disconcerting!
I thought wisdom suffused the old.

My voice grows rustier, less dependable.
"A natural part of aging,"
says my ENT specialist.
"The vocal folds don't close
as well as they once did."

Always accident-prone
I now fall more easily, and when
I attribute this to some dark
psychological etiology
I'm assured it's what happens when...

My nearly-smooth-as-ever face belies
wrinkles crisscrossing my body.
All I have to do to find
an expert who knows about wrinkles
is mention them to friends. You guessed it!

Funny! Nobody suggests age
as the reason I can laugh at myself now
always a sobersides before.
I've learned to survive loss by floating—
until will and strength flow once more.

Up

It isn't often
I get a full-blown
view of who I am, what
I'm about.

This morning, grabbing
that last few minutes of sleep
I become a balloon, yellow
with random blue swirls

wafting comfortably   up
above the real world
into a cloudless
sky. I easily top

mountains   which flatten
out below me   and tiny
ribbons winding without
effort around all obstacles

even as I   now float free
then plunge purposefully ahead.
On the way up. Content to take my time.
Descent? I've never heard the word.

Down

When I first moved to this twelfth-floor apartment
I wondered if there might come a time when I
would hesitate to stand on my narrow balcony lest
I look down   and be tempted to simply fling
myself over that easily surmounted barrier, a time
when the complexity of living   the immense
tendency of humans to repeat past errors   regardless
of awareness   inflexibility and resistance
to change   the fear, too, of a drawn-out diminishing
of power to plan my own life   when all these
might suddenly overwhelm me   and I might seek an easy
way of eliminating them and me all at one blow.
The minute the word *easy* drifted into consciousness
I knew no matter how down I might get I'd never do it.
Easy for me possibly   but for those I love   years of
wondering   perhaps self-blame   resentment.
The image of each one of them returns me safely to sanity.

I Seem to Be Turning

into the kind of older person
who enjoys passing on
wise words
to those following me, crystalline
words that will provide essence
of blue and yellow
essential to avoid grey smudges,
lead neophytes safely through the maze
all of us face daily. I know
yet am prone to forget
we need to discover
most of life for ourselves.

Talking Stone

Our leader passes around stones
in a woven basket decorated
with a ring of interlocking hatchets.
He invites us to find ourselves
within these earth fragments.

You seek my hand almost before
I see you clearly. You do not speak
to me at all though I have rescued you
from oblivion. Smooth and flat
on one side, my first attraction palls
after a few minutes. You seem
totally drained of emotion, reminding me
of another whose face reveals little
of what boils within. And my mirrored
face shows one bland side.

Held away from me, catching only
the contour of your face   I see
a pleasant enough older person
the least quirk of a smile.
But then I hold you close
and find the smile seems more
a ghastly grin—remnant perhaps
of your struggle to cling
to a world no longer yours,
sadness at a world so soon lost?

"Any reaction from yours yet?"
whispers my next-seat neighbor
with the smirk of a nonbeliever.

"Oh yes, we've been having a lively
conversation," I reply, only half in jest.
I have just observed that crack
down one cheek. The hidden anger
the sudden blow across the face. I can feel
it now   after all these years.

Summer Solstice

When I was growing up
in northern Wisconsin, I knew little
about summer or winter solstices.

I did know about my Dad's small garden,
planted each spring after late frost,
he always hoped, was seldom wrong.

We ate suppers in our backyard
close to Dad's rows of sweet radishes
curly green and butter lettuce,

Swiss chard, of course, and asparagus.
I was our asparagus harvester, testing each
tender stalk to find just that point

of stubborn resistance. My sister Ruth
and I, or my mother and I after Ruth had left
to be a grown-up, sat companionably close on cool

crisp mornings under the oak, shucked tiny peas
from their pods, shucking too whatever rancor
was left over from the day before.

Dad raised a few flowers—bleeding hearts and
lilies of the valley, violets. He added pansies
and zinnias as the perennials went to their rest.

But his love was for vegetables, for growing food
that helped his family grow, gave him a sense
of being a farmer like his father before him.

Why Flowers Bloom

When I was a little girl
I used to think
I could make flowers bloom
simply by loving them—
violets, tulips, even roses.
I got this idea one spring
when I noticed how
each delicate or sturdy flower
in my father's garden
came up the same time each spring
about the time I began to look for them.

How I bloomed in the warmth
I felt from my father,
his quiet way of making me feel
important and unique.
And later, when my Bill and I
chose each other, how my hair shone
my eyes looked out proudly
instead of turning away
in recurring shyness.
Then there was the first time each of our twin sons
decided I was someone close and
turned to me for nurturing.

Tonight, coming away from a reading
where I felt the audience
and I had connected—
mostly young women, eager, empathic
with a sprinkling of intrepid young men—

I could feel their response
and my response to them
so that with each new poem
I gained new strength, new willingness
to share my life and feelings
before it is my time
to return once more
to dark, warm mother earth.

Love surely is the answer
no matter the kind, no matter the source.

Planting Young Birch Trees

(in honor of National Arbor Day)

Through the woods rimming
Planting Ground Lake, a cluster
of birch trees glisten in morning sun

a light sprinkle of snow, last
of the winter, we hope, outlines
their slender branches. White on white.

Like all trees, the birch seem
eager to reach the sky. Arms
stretch high, wave down at anyone

following the trail from cottage
to lake. Gone now the pink arbutus,
Johnny-jump-ups, wild columbine—

hidden beneath the snow. All nature
seems to be waiting for me
to signal the new season

by planting my ten young birch trees.

Defensive Tactics

On my balcony
few plants survive
the wind and strong sun.

A palm tree I'd raised
from a date seed, pampered pet,
developed a tough hide

when I placed it on my aerie.
A spider matriarch, used
to vicissitudes, permitted

a single leaf to brown, remained
intact herself, babies and all.
My jade plant, never a user

of water, did fine the first
few weeks, suddenly turned
bright red. Naturally, I tried

giving it a drink. Within
minutes, it returned
to its usual brilliant jade.

I admire my plants' defensive
tactics. Perhaps I'll not need
to convert to geraniums, after all.

Vision

For a second time   I have this image
of objects   bulging almost human shapes
some dark   in somber tones
others so transcendentally light
they seem to shine
a few with a kind of bark
shaggy   surely not like any human form
and yet not unlike either.
All appear to be only half
of what they had been   perhaps could be
again   when   as they are drawn
across my vision   by some preternatural force
passing over a still forest-ringed lake
my objects take on a wholeness   almost
holiness   for but an instant   as they
pass over the water below   before moving
beyond   into dark   and beyond my ken.

For Those Who Want to Experience Everything

Don Quixote, that windmill tilter,
my husband's favorite hero,
came to me tonight
in a dream.
Stop   he warned me.
find a couple of good windmills.
Devote yourself to them.
Give up all others.

As Don drifted away, a photographer
I once knew well appeared,
reminded me of selective focus,
darling of photographers
who wanted to cope with busyness:
two or maybe three giant trees instead of one.
Soften that background, he told me.
Why so many competing, conflicting images?

By now, I was beginning to get
a message, written in **BOLD** and **CAPS**
clearly an attention getter.
A large cup came on my screen
filled to brimming.
Your cup runneth over, intoned
a voice straight out of my youth.

At first these visions had come
separately. But now they clamored
loudly to be heard, all jumbled together
dressed in changing, brilliant colors
with flashing lights and fragments
unrelated to one another.
Out of this tangle
a thunderous voice. *Listen to me. SLOW DOWN.*

Point of View

Straight ahead
or around—
our usual ways of looking.

Up at times of stress.
Not sure anyone is up there
we sometimes turn our gaze inward,

which can symbolize despair.

Now that I live high up
I look down and around—
which makes everyone

and everything
seem different
smaller. Farther away.

Sometimes, I still look up
more out of habit
than belief.

More often I listen closely
to what's happening
within.

I like to hear the purring.

Playing Games

My fine insurance company and I
are playing games with each other.
As my insurance broker hands me
my new Nursing Home Policy
complete with Home Health Rider
he assures me solemnly I'll never
need a nursing home as long
as I have this policy.
With solemnity to match his
I tell him I am convinced, now
I have this fine umbrella, surely
no rain will fall. Both of us
hope we're right. A win/win situation!
I'd gladly swap my annual premium
for surety I'll die quietly
in my own bed.

Peace Poem

(for Maya Angelou)

In her deep voice—perhaps a gift
from those five years she chose
to be mute—she tells us
one thing I'll keep beneath my pillow,
bring out on some of these dark nights
our world seems determined to self-destruct:

"Remember," she says,
"the many ways all of us are alike,
the very few in which we differ."

This morning, early, I
tote them up, those similarities.
We think (or try to), make mistakes,
eat, sleep, make love, feel touched
by nature's shapes and colors, movement.
Out of these we create poems, art, music.
We relish stories of another's
misery and joy, our own small successes.
All of us die after brief or protracted pain
yearn to leave only when confident
at least a few will regret our passing.

The ways we differ seem too few
too inconsequential
to bother mentioning.

Thirteen at Three-Thirty A.M.

I wakened with a great idea for a poem.
Each line marched into view
precise and military
as foreign soldiers.
Alas
before I could put a single
word to paper
the meaning
escaped me. Sometimes life
is like that, it seems—
all form and formality
too little going on
of real substance.

City

Oh sing me a song of a city asleep
night sounds and purring silences.

The steady thrum of my apartment building
warming, protecting its people.

Twelve stories below me, two palm trees
shiver in their shallow roots, listen anxiously

for first splatter of rain, moaning
urging heavy clouds to drop their burdens.

Out of nowhere a fire truck blasts
down the street, two, three—must be a big one.

I pick my way around piles of papers
get to my balcony in time to see red taillights.

Still the warning lingers. From my balcony
I watch a sprinkle of lights, dim shapes, slant rooftops.

In the distance, a half circle wavers in midair
as a single car stitches and outlines the dark freeway.

When I sniff the air, I sense, even this high,
a faint odor of earth before rains come to bless.

Last Blooming

Remember from your gardening days—
or if you've not yet discovered
the joys of acting midwife
to flowers and vegetables,
from some earlier time when you
watched a parent bent over a hoe,
how flowers have a way
of telling when to spend
their bloom with such fulsome beauty—
it seemed as if there never had been
a lovelier hyacinth or daffodil
nor so many blossoms, often a sudden burst
of flowering when you had thought your favorite
Talisman rose or lily of the valley
through blooming for this season?
I always felt there was something urgent
about this last show of color and fragrance,
that somehow the flower knew
if she did not burst into glory
this one more time it would be all over.

I feel that urgency as I sit here
listen to my second poem this morning demand
that I give it voice *right now.*

Planting

is hard work.
First you till the field
or whatever small plot.
You may not have tools
that break the soil.
You may run into hardpan.
That can set you back weeks
sometimes years. Try
dynamite. Or another field.
Then break the earth up
with your hands if necessary
until it is fine and porous
so water and light can get through.
Finally, a little fertilizer
around each hollowed-out hole.
And remember. Do not
plant stones.
Only seeds.

Mr. Death

(for William and Sasha and all children who wonder about death)

A pretty sight he was—Mr. Death in his top hat
his white bones and his high-top shoes
all dressed up for his nightly spin
in his spring-green wagon.
His faithful mule, Nellie, like her
mother before her, spent her years
going cloppity-clop along the roads
and lanes and streets and avenues
of the world, wherever Mr. Death
told her to go. Every single night at dusk.

Mr. Death sat up front, of course.
The back of the wagon was partitioned
into small, medium, and large
rectangles, all comfortably cushioned
ready to receive. A few tall, skinny
compartments.

Now and then Mr. Death would remind Nellie
to slow and she slowed to a stop,
always at the right door.
A smart mule, Nellie.
So all Mr. Death had to do
was to knock gently on the door.
Of course, sometimes people
who were not ready tried
not answering but this never worked
for long—if they failed
to answer this time, he would
pick them up on his next spin their way.

Babies liked to hear Mr. Death's friendly
voice when they had been hurting.
Old people who had lived a long and full
life rarely put up much of a fuss.
Some old people needed a bit of cajoling—
they'd gotten used to the idea they might live
forever—but he gentled them out the door.

When he had a full load—every soft-cushioned
compartment filled—Mr. Death clucked softly
to Nellie, and off they went, more slowly
now because of Nellie's heavy load.
"That's a good girl," Mr. Death comforted her.
"No use to hurry. We'll soon be home
and you can rest all day. I've planned
a special treat for you. A red juicy apple."
Nellie's long ears flapped appreciatively.
Soon she and her passengers were home,
just as the sun's early beams flickered
through the trees in all the forests of the world
then flooded the earth. A new day began.

Jet Lag

is when you've been on a trip
where the time is out of whack—
either faster or slower
by three hours   or even eight
so what would be time for getting up
is really time to turn in
by the new time   or other way around
then   just as you almost get the hang
of it   your lovely   sometimes terrible
or lovely/terrible trip's over
and you're *home*
again.

Now   breakfast is when
it used to be   and going to work
is the time it always was
same way for playtime   only
because you've been on that trip
lovely, terrible, or lovely/terrible
everything feels unreal
spacey.

How to come down without crashing?
My secret: act *as if* for awhile   *pretend*
you're back to what used to be your reality
when time was manageable   stayed put.
try getting up with *our roosters*
going off to school or work when neighbors
do   save playtime for *our dark time.*

Pretty soon   maybe sooner than you think possible
you'll be one of us once more.   Trick
is   take note of when the roosters crow
right where you find
yourself.

True Love Never

runs smooth, they used to say.
Now people talk less about love
more about a caring relationship.
Well, that doesn't run downhill
all the time either.

At least we can learn something
from every blowup. Like what brought
this one? Was it like the last?
If different, how different?
No use looking for who's to blame—

it's always both of us, so why bother?
The simplest way, I ruefully decide,
now I'm back to my old confident self,
is first look within me and *then* at you.
But think of all the fiery poems I'd lose!

If It Seems Strange

to you and you and you
perhaps even to You, my New Friend,
as it does sometimes to me
that   at a time when others
are following the ways of the world
so different these days
from every other time,
whole countries breaking apart
one part turning against another
trying out new combinations of power—
like a sea of mighty icebergs
crashing against each other
once they have broken from their mother—
concentrating too on how we can fit
into a world so vastly changed   especially
how we will spend what surely will be
a Dividend of Peace   one of these days—
at such a time I   who used to be
a happily married woman
enjoying my life with my husband
but surely not more focused on sex
than the rest of you   strange I now
spend much of my waking time
and more of my dreaming hours
in experiencing renewed sensations
as my body suddenly lets me know
it is safe again to feel as other women
perhaps not for long but at least
for now. If all this seems strange

to you   as it does to me   I have only
to remember that time when feelings
of love and pure pleasure in another
were suddenly pinched off   like a blossom
rudely torn away from its stem.
That blossom is gone forever
yet the plant lives on   craves nourishment.

Oh! Those Lovely Vowel Sounds

If, instead of spending thirty years
trying to help people
understand themselves and others
I had been a linguist, reveling
in all those lovely vowel sounds
I might not have wasted so much time
wondering why
I compulsively repeated
time after boring time
words like *Boutros Boutros-Galli*
or *achingly* or *Boutolasi*—
which seemed to have no
relevance to me
but only served, I thought,
to keep me from finding
whatever word or image
actually troubled me.

How simple, to realize these words
have value in themselves, not
necessarily only a screen
designed to hide unconscious
from conscious self.

I might, too,
have become a "pure poet."
Much as some painters choose
color and form

without thought for meaning
only dominance and contrast,
I would use words that loll or roll
around my mouth, pleasuring
my tongue and love of words.

Retired Writer's Window of Opportunity

"When's the best time to phone you?"
asked my new friend.

"Never in the morning," I replied.
"That's when I write."

"How about early afternoon?"

"Afternoon's are sort of iffy.
I usually go to a writer's group. Or shop."

"Well then, right after you get home?"

"Not before dinner. My nap. I'd bite your head off.
And of course *McNeil/Lehrer* at six-thirty."

"I never heard of anyone more inaccessible!"
he said. "Are you sure you *want* me to call?"

"Of course I do! Oh, I know! Call me
between seven-thirty and eight.

"Before all my favorite programs. *Nova. P.O.V.*
That's like a little window of opportunity."

"That," he said firmly, banging the door
on his way out, "is when I take *my* nap."

Attraction

is a funny thing.
How would I know my father's

blue eyes and rare smile,
his stolid steadiness

Uncle Herschel's handlebar mustache
(circa 1920), his courtly manners

Robert what-was-his-name-anyway
who took me to the junior prom

my first psychology teacher, white-
bearded, forgetting the word

when he lectured about amnesia
(his features frozen in a single stance)

even my husband's brooding face, dark eyes
and wonderful black eyebrows

his love of sitting on a thorny fence
his special musky odor

would combine somehow to make me turn
and melt toward you all these years later?

On Staying Out

Coming out
from a cocoon of shyness
bursting forth
from that tight swaddle
parents of girls used
to bind about us—
"nice little girls are seen,
not heard"—finally, we make it, then find
we're apt to be garrulous at times
talking and talking and talking
for pure joy of feeling free
to share what's been within.

Then a gentleman of the old school
tries to put us back into his
idea of a woman's place
implying, or even saying, "You talk too much!"
That's the time to tell yourself you're glad you're not
his nor anyone's little girl,
keep right on talking.
You'll slow down when you're ready,
as a rusty bell, freed from enforced silence,
first loudly clangs in exultation
eventually yearns to also hear
the sweet chime of other voices.

When to Abandon a Banana

All of us are taught to tell a bad
apple. Brown, squishy soft. Toss it!

A banana, like humans, is susceptible
to spoiling of a subtler sort.
Take this yellow fellow, glowing
in the sun of your fond gaze.
It may show no blemish on its skin
at most a black or bluish bruise
close to where banana joins parent stalk.
Looks like a body blow.

Peel back one flap of protective cover
two   a third   and you're in.

Only firm flesh the color of cream
with the first bite. Even the third
if you're lucky. As you near that bruise
a tiny dark spot. Follow to its source.
As you tunnel down   you'll see the spread
of corruption. Down the darkened mass you go.
Metastasis is an ugly thing.

At some point soon   you'll need to decide
whether you must give up on your unwise choice.

Transitions

This is the night
I found myself dreaming
in brush strokes

after nearly two decades
of dreaming in images, similes
metaphors and symbols.

First, the poems slowed
to a molasses drip.
Then dreams stopped altogether.

Oh, they were there, deep
within my unconscious.
Inaccessible to me.

Same thing happened when I moved
from photography to poem making
then briefly, recently, and

years later, from narrative poetry
to recounting little stories. So why
should I be surprised

when I woke to discover
my right hand stroking the air
trying to decide if a mauve hat

suited my heroine better than yellow.

Totem Change

Long ago I gave up
on that first of my totems
the straight line. Alas
it so rarely seemed
to fulfill its promise
of being the shortest distance
from me to anyone else.

For years, I have thought
the circle—that ritual emblem
of ancient goddesses,
with so many female meanings:
coming together of two bodies
sometimes souls as well,
egg, uterus, rounding
of swollen belly as months complete
their appointed time, the birth/death
circle itself—might represent me.
Yet when a circle is broken
rudely, without my acquiescence,
what have we then? Only
a poor thing, forced to begin
the long search for another half.

How different from both is the spiral!
I am filled with wonder—
the power, the freedom. What other path
could constantly renew us, let
us find a surprise around each curving
sinuous twist in our road, keep until
the very end the intricacies of our lives?

I marvel at the ear, and its counterpart
the shell, each so delicate, contrived.
The tortuous writhings of snakes, their speed.
That forest mountain stream rushing
to join the sea, as we to our spirit.
That anyone may join us at any time
leave when it suits us both,
travel upward or downward as we choose.

Gemini

We Gemini run a constant risk
of bumping into ourselves
as we reverse twin courses.

Sometimes I think people
with schizophrenia, that illness
where absolute ambivalence is alleged

to hold sway, must all be Gemini,
so strong is the two-sidedness roiling
about in only one body/mind.

Take this poem. Any poem. I can
start out looking outside and inside
myself at a single subject   like schizophrenia.

All at once, a dozen
other subjects rear up like throaty frogs
bellowing for equal time.

Eventually I can wrestle these down
to two often totally unrelated supplicants
and if I'm lucky, back to schizophrenia.

I'd like to blame this on the accident
of being born on June 15. Or is schizophrenia
simply what it's like to be a poet?

Nouveau Peacock

If you have an older woman friend
who suddenly discovers a new
interest in her wardrobe, begins
to frequent women's specialty shops,
comes home with dresses, jackets
even dress trousers in teal, fuchsia, and purple
and to appear in these gorgeous, almost-
inappropriate raiments   before you
conclude she has taken leave
of her senses and wonder if big
floppy hats and white gloves
are next,
ask yourself why she has given up soft greens
and blues, durable sports clothes
so late in her life.

Where was she, for instance,
during the Great Depression? Could it be
she and her new husband made do on
one hundred a month or less?
That they were cooped up
in a tiny
one-purpose room
in a run-down neighborhood?
No car, of course.
Mostly oatmeal, carrots, and casseroles,
with pot roast on Sunday to last until Thursday.

Relatives sent packets of hand-me-downs
in browns and greys, not colors of her choosing.
To keep the packets coming, she wrote
letters of thanks to the donors.

Be kind. Tell your friend she looks great in purple.

Intimacy Is Not

purely sexual
transmuting though that is
I remember.

The best times
we talked quietly
in the dark of our bed

quietly, lest we wake
our two young sons
and suddenly the focus

would be changed. We reveled
in being parents of twins
until our bedtime.

Nights, we felt, should still
be ours. A special aura
surrounded the two of us

encircling us in intimacy.
With the first wail
we turned into family

more parents than lovers.
You, too, know both kinds of joy.

Maple on Fire

Looming before me elegant and graceful, a woman
long hair shimmering in late sun
the strands variegated.
I can almost smell
the odor of burnt leaves,
feel of rake beneath my mittened hands,
watch leaves flutter down   or in a wind
great flurries roaring to earth.
They can hardly wait to join the others
soft interweaving   all feeling of individuality lost
one and only one   and then none.

A long time since I have lived
close to maple trees in autumn.
I had forgotten how they can lift the spirits
make me believe in color   magic   change.

They lure me with impermanence
making me do things I had not known
I wanted to do   like asking a man
for dinner   not once but twice
and I keep wondering   he is still green
in color   yet silent   like a towering pine
and I am more like the maples   I flair up in fall
before I leave   go down again into the earth.

Slow and Fast Time

Time seemed elastic
as a rubber band
when I was young.

If something fun
was coming up
time galloped.

Doing a hated chore
could make time seem
like forever.

Same way now I'm older
only different. Most days
time ambles along

one day not too unlike
the last or the next.
But if someone I love

is coming for a visit
time can become starlit
speedy as light.

Nothing heals as fast
now I am older   so when
I'm hurt   time lags

and if the hurt is caused
by loss of a mate or a son
or daughter or grandchild

that pain can linger
long past the time others
think I *ought* to mourn.

Skipping Stones

You and I
unagitated lake or surging stream
search   right stones—
glass-flat
smooth to hand.
        SKIP   SPLASH
              SKIP   splash
                    skip-skip-skip   tiny splash.
How many this time?

Now I skip stones   alone.
Trick is   save out one stone
for my final   last   splash.

Coming Out

Remember how it felt
when you came out
as a woman
how scary—everyone
would learn you too were smart?

Then those who love
people of their own sex
came out and found
they'd lost only
a heavy burden, not their pride.

Now I, at eighty,
have decided to let the world
know I have big ears.
Worse, the right one is slightly bent.
"Your grandpa's ears," my mother disparaged.

Today my new and daring barber
taught me, snipping away,
my ears look pretty much like
most ears, only a tad more distinctive.
And I seem to have grown into them.

As if a rabbit with an outsize pair
belatedly realizing
her ears were an integral part of her
confidently let them float in the breeze
or stream behind in ecstasy.

Moon Shining in at Four A.M.

Last night, I was one of a panel
of older folks—two women, three men

told gerontology students what it's like
to grow older. We ranged widely, ended up with sex.

In all the months I've lived at my
retirement place never before

has the moon looked directly in on me.
Yet here she is, benignly smiling

down, reminding me of that summer
before you died, when we spent

so many nights together as you photographed
the crescent moon, moon at one quarter,

half grown, three quarters. When at her
fullest, you spent hours getting precisely

the pose you wanted, almost as if you
realized you would be up there with her in

another few months. You felt her smiling
encouragement to you as I now feel she smiles at me.

Last night on TV I watched as
Sylvia Plath read her moon poem

then her daddy poem, and I'm glad
all over again that I no longer

feel bonded to my father, nor even to you
my husband. Keep on looking for someone alive

murmurs the moon. Surely there is a lively
eighty-year-old man who's watching, too, somewhere.

No use wasting the stirrings that wakened me
on someone not here to enjoy them—and me.

Query Letter to My Sister Poets

I'm curious.
Are you too influenced
by tides of the moon
long after your years of childbearing?
Do you too find yourselves
waking   each night she shows herself
and especially when she is at her fullest?
Do you feel bursting to get some phrase   or phase
of your life down on paper
so as not to lose it?
I say, sister poets! Surely I am not the only one?

The Female Body

For many years, young females
need pay no mind to their bodies.
Their very female curves are dependably
there and theirs and available
to admire and dress and share.

Now that I am older, I find myself
aware of each change, the sags and wrinkles.
The subtle ways we no longer look
like ourselves. Those deep valleys
where body joins arms and legs!
Surely never there before.
The way our eyes sink back into sockets.

Yet aware, too, that we are not beyond
small changes in the opposite direction.
Let a new man come into my life
and all my senses quiver, my eyes
take on rekindled sparkle, my breasts perk up.

Dancing at the Senior Center

Today   first time
in maybe fifty years
(for me) a friend
and I went dancing.
We practiced
on my apartment's orange rug
the waltz-two-three
the determinedly foxy fox-trot
and a lively Polish dance.
"You're doing fine," my friend
encouraged. "Just loosen up a bit.
Let me do the leading."

How let another lead me
when I've spent seven long years
learning to steer myself?

Then all at once it came
and we were gliding
together.

Most of my marriage   my husband
couldn't dance   his game leg
made it torture   even
the sensual close-up dancing
to "The Blue Room" we used to love.

He claimed he didn't miss it.
"Never mind. We don't need
to dance   now we're married."
But I did mind   tried to steer
myself about the house.

Strange now   to find pleasure
in another's leading me.

Listening to DeBussy's *La Mer*

While Doing Something Else

First   the swell and surge
then silky flow of strings.
A kind of playfulness.
Now the movement quickens
builds with thrusting rhythm
until a *crash*
and then retreats
to quiet beach   oh, so slowly
builds again to higher, higher peak
slips down to momentary pause.
An undercurrent of sadness.
Only two lovers
could truly listen
while doing something else.

Twelve William Turner Watercolors

(in appreciation of a William Turner landscape calendar)

Just when winter is most dank
here is this glowing scene—
two repeating clefts between two cliffs
the closer one shadowed at its base,
a dip in the distance leveled by constant
flow and pressure   water
plumes pour over a high fall.

One man toils up the near cliff, a couple
enjoy a lark   tiny humans
sharp   in an otherwise dreamy
sweep of earth. Two cows—one surveys me,
the other readies herself to follow sister
cows up the steep hill. Seven oblivious sheep
point the way to the waterfall.

I find it hard to turn the page to February
until I find William Turner's ancient street scene—
early travelers alighting from coaches in a town square,
sun only now striking onions and spires.
Why does Turner draw me so? Is it the vastness
of his landscapes? Simple themes? Or is it because
each human is actively engaged, coping, learning to cope?

Because It Is Nine Months

we have known each other
I want to say to you—
you have become dear to me.
You know how a favorite friend
is valued? Without acute
scrutiny, without a wish
to charm, without
even, a need to label—
only this feeling
of empathy and caring,
of joy when I hear your voice
see you at my door
posies in hand,
especially as we confide
in each other, plumb
depths and crannies
we sometimes did not know
were within us. Love is not
the word. Too simple
and at once too complex.

Babies often take
a few days more than nine months
so why should we
not take our time

to discover
how and why we care?
And if we end up
not knowing
the precise word,
what's in a word? Enough
to realize that for this day
you are one added reason
for me to enjoy living—
want to live a little longer.

Prayer by a Naïf

Please, God, if I
have in my long life
been faithful in Thy sight
wilt Thou remember this
at the time of my death
so that it may be pain free
or at least
with no more pain than Thou feel
right for one with my good intentions.
And may it be, O God, as short
as Thou canst contrive.
Naturally, God, I hope and fully believe
that Thou wilt put off my death
for as long a time as Thou feel
fair for one so pure in heart.
I thank Thee, God,
for hearing my plea.

Faint Aroma of Chicken Soup

In the middle of a sodden sleep
heavy   seemingly dreamless
this phrase kept waking me.

At first it made no sense.
All day the day before I'd watched
fascinated   horrified   like you

as first a young woman told
of sexual harassment   then the accused
harasser   having decided attack

was his best   indeed his only defense
gave the lie to all accusations
claimed not to have watched TV that day.

Like other women   as I listened
to her   I thought back   to my sole
experience with harassment.

I was twelve   maybe thirteen
and blossoming. My best friend's father
had been teaching me to swim.

Suddenly   his body became electric
demanding   of what I had no idea.
We were in deep water. I could barely

swim a stroke alone. For weeks I dreamed
of how I felt   father-person
one minute   demanding stranger the next.

Don't listen when they say   with a smirk,
"Men never make passes at girls
who wear glasses."

I still remember   though faintly now
how nausea engulfed me   when my friend's
mother had chicken soup waiting for us.

Sixty-some years have passed since then.
I told no one for ten   and only
as Personal Story in a creative writing class.

Turtling: The Action or Process of Catching Turtles

Holding up a small toy turtle so all
of us could see, the psychiatric consultant
commented: "Self-punishment is a strange thing."

"Someone tell me—what does this
remind you of?" Forgetting I was new
or that I was speaking out in a huge crowd

of other social workers, I leaped up, called out
"That's the shell I put over my head
when I was five. 'You *should* know better,'

my mother told me, slapping my face.
'After all we've done to teach you right
from wrong, you *should* know. A big girl now.'

"I put those *shoulds* right over my head.
Like a shell." I was sobbing now, tears streaming.
Freedom was right around

this corner. I felt that *should* slip
off my shoulders, stomped it into a murky pool.
The psychiatric consultant thanked me

and moved on, this time holding up a tiny cage.
"Which of you has put yourself
behind these bars?" he asked.

Separation

"Just separate the baby from its mother,"
said my next-door neighbor, an expert
on indoor plants. "Slice it right off, then
shore up the dirt around the big plant
and fix the young a nice bed
of its own. They'll each do better."

Slicing turned out to be a greater chore
than I'd anticipated. I hacked away, murmuring
soothingly to both as I worked. As I completed
the separation process, I remembered a boy
I'd placed in a foster home. And then another
and another. He never did forget

the feel of that first sharp thrust, being twisted
away from all he knew and loved. I wonder
where he is now, whether he ever found
someone who could give him the same
feeling of being part of something bigger
than himself. Or is he still searching?

Bright Yellow Bowl

Yesterday, your
bright yellow bowl (for blended clam)
your dish of patterned blue on white
(to set off nubbins of Ocean Fish)
were fixtures in my cheerful kitchen.
We were companions
for eight years. Together
we survived the move from country home
to condominium apartment, though you
spent most of the first six months
sleeping. Each time of wakening
you leaped up joyfully, sure
your master had returned
and we were home again.
Now another moving time has come.
This time cats are not allowed.
No answer to my ad inviting
a lonely person to become your mother.
Yesterday, I took you back to where
you'd been reared, watched you wind your tail
about the leg of the new owner of our former home.
"I don't think you need to worry
about Blackie," he said, leaning down
to scratch your ear, peer into your golden eyes.
"Come any time to visit."

Unplotted

After a lifetime of plotting
my course   looking ahead
to the next grade

the new job   the eager marriage
to getting a raise   bearing
and raising our sons

health taken for granted
young   and hopeful   enough to be able
to share with those coming after

now seems a time
for sudden and murky blindness. No longer
can I predict my future

as if a plotter of weather   or maps
suddenly lost his or her bearings
compass or pen unbelievably lost

only that pinpoint of darkness ahead
the one we all reach in our own time.
This is a time   if ever

for finding my joy for the day
in a grandchild's welcoming smile
in one more day I had no fall nor close call

one more twenty-four-hour span
when I can enjoy my good fortune
a pulse still beating away at my dreams.

Yin and Yang in Retirement

communities only faintly
resemble relationships I remember
from on the outside.

There, we met the opposite sex
at school or work or play
or maybe sang together
in the church choir
had a chance to see a man
busy at something he
loved or hated or only tolerated
before we let on yes, we
found him attractive, too.

Here, cooped up together
in our twelve-floor high-rise
sharing meals and an elevator
there's no place to hide. If
one of us feels even a spark
of something, everyone around us is sure
to sniff it out, sometimes before
the message gets to the one intended.
Marital status is often blurred.

Gradually we find out which men
flirt with all the women, especially
the needy ones, like compassionate
older brothers taking wallflower
sisters to a dance. We can observe

how the man who just moved in to #1100
handles being new, fight or flight.
Is he a modest robin or noisy seagull?
Watch him in the laundry: competent or playing Poor Me?

Decisions that might take us months
even years outside are often made here
with one blink of our jaded yet still eager eyes.

Stepping Out

Living downtown
as we do   fire truck's clang
comes at us by day, more often by night.

We who live on the top floor
have learned to ignore these alarums
blend them in with other city noises.

All except the imperious shriek of the ambulance.
We can be quietly eating lunch in our dining room
when chewing stops   and conversation.

Where will the paramedics go this time?
Is it our neighbor Sarah, feeling ill last night?
Last week one of our men residents was bashed

over the head with a wine bottle by a reeling man
who demanded change for a twenty, attacking the older man
as he left the bus. His face is still a mottled purple.

Yesterday another friend, moved in only ten days ago,
all hope and cheer, was carried out on a stretcher.
Today, will I be the one to trip on my orange rug

as I whirl about my living room, avoiding furniture
caught up in the rhythms of Ravel's *Bolero?* Carefully
as we step, death comes. I'd like death to find me whirling.

Numbers Nightmare

I am standing in front of a theater
selling tickets for nine dollars
and ninety-seven cents. The crowd
packs in as if they were buying
tickets for a longer life.
Maybe they are.

All at once I realize I have charged
two cents too little. This seems
of monumental importance.
I produce a scarlet pail, impossible
to ignore as viewers stream homeward
after the show. I attach a big sign
asking them, as a matter of honor,
to drop two cents in the bucket,
explaining my undercharging.

Nobody complies. They no longer carry
small change. They ignore me.
One woman makes out a check
for two cents, ostentatiously drops
it in. She grimaces, letting me know
she thinks I'm a tightwad.
Finally, I decide to charge my loss
to Profit and Loss.

Before I leave
I must see what the show
was all about, learn the big secret.
Just as I open the door
to the now empty theater
the lights go off.
Frustrated, I turn to leave
inadvertently   kick the bucket.

New Generation of Warriors

In between the reporting general's
recital of number of sorties,
objectives sighted and destroyed,
an announcement: the military
toy business is booming.
Why should that surprise us?

Families with both father and mother
now engaged in war
surely will talk up
their bravery, the hardships,
how proud the little boy—or girl—
should feel to have both parents
in the war. If the mother is still
home with the children, how glad
she'll be to have a military toy they
can use to play war, "just like Daddy."

And so, quite naturally, the next
generation of warriors
will be drawn all unwittingly
into assuming one day she or he will go to war.

How innate the bee's busyness, the lioness's
strong maternal instincts. Only humans
seem to build into our universal psyches
a need to kill our own kind. When will peace
be as fixed, as impervious to assault
as are these animal instincts?

Mesmerizing

these words of war or near-war—
what we were used to
all those years.
"And who will gain
in this waiting game?" asks
the interviewer. "Iraq—
or the U.S.?" Only the names
have changed. Soon there may be
casualties, one side or other
then both. Only a step
from that to the daily count
to the drone of words
designed to make us forget
we had been so close
to peace.

Death in the Family

All morning I've felt down
as if someone close to me
his name unknown
had died.

Yet surely   if he
were close I would remember
who he is   or was.
At first I thought

my memory lapse
might be because
the one deceased
no longer conscious

able to speak
or even to cry out the moment
he lost touch with all of us
might be one I had known

at some earlier time
whose name had slipped
into the abyss I discover
more and more often these days.

Yet a search dredged up nobody.
Perhaps a former patient
I had known in group therapy
whose name had disappeared?

All at once his name hit me
with the force of a blow—the man
who finally was executed at dawn
after a night of repeated reprieves.

And I had not even written a letter.
No wonder I repressed his name!

I believe even a person
convicted of killing two
should not be felled
by the state which held him

on Death Row all these years.
All I feel now
is a dull despair.
Flashes of black rage.

How can his death by all of us
make another man feel more human?

Outsider

Two weeks I've waited
to feel the time was right
to visit the Quilt display—
that collection of people's lives
and feelings, crafted with love
and vivid colors, memories
of men/women related by blood or caring
to the quilter, patient stitches
salted by tears, hot, resentful
of young life snuffed out
by a killer not yet at bay—
waited and each day decided tomorrow
might be better, today being stuffed
too full already. Or maybe this weekend?

What was I waiting for? For whom?
Someone to say, "Let's go, shall we?"
Why would I need that? I, a volunteer
at the AIDS foundation, surely
should feel this ritual visit
this payment of homage to the lost
and to those who remember was my right, my
obligation. Why? Why? As the day
for closing the exhibition neared,
I tried to push myself to go, failed,
felt somehow I had no right to share
such private pain.

Too late, I've come to realize
the pain belongs to each of us.

In Celebration of Earthweek, 1990

How terrible if you and I had not lived
to see whole countries rise up

almost as one body to demand freedom
of choice! Did you ever think

you might live long enough to watch, fascinated,
as one government after another acknowledged

dark crimes stoutly denied for years?
Perhaps both of us—you, young; I, old—

may yet see a day when the world is
peopled with folks who are *for* the environment,

and the word *enemy* is obsolete. When peace
is taken for granted, and the common good

is what drives us, not grubby greed.
When our young are drawn by love of nature

no longer need wars—or drugs—to fuel
feelings of kinship with each other.

More Blessed

My friend Ed, through several nightmare
misadventures, found himself
in an empty apartment
without immediate funds to buy furniture.
His predicament made me wish I could help.
"I don't have an extra bed or chairs,"
I told him, "but I'll see what I have to share."

I spent a pleasant Sunday making choices.
One sheet, a few towels, wheat-color thermal blanket.
Three yellow dishes, all I had left
of a favorite Italian set.
Maybe that yellow will cheer Ed on gloomy
winter days, I thought. Image of Ed's long legs
wrapped around a kitchen chair as he
enjoyed bagels, coffee, and Cheerios.

Then I went through my store of magazines
hoarded for that mythical time
when I'd have more leisure for perusal,
chose those I thought might appeal
to Ed's eclectic interests.

Another friend agreed to drop off my two boxes—
if we could do it Wednesday.
No telephone, so I'd have to risk
missing Ed. My driver friend added an intrusion—
a sturdy but ugly umbrella, poked it
into one corner of a box. I felt like asking
her to take it out, was stopped by feeling beholden.

Nobody home. I wished I'd brought paper
for a note. "From my house to your house,"
my mother used to write when sharing with friends.

I didn't hear from Ed right away, almost
concluded the boxes had been seized
by a passerby, when Ed phoned.
He was upset, though not sure why. Someone
had implied he might be a second-class citizen.

It was only after we hung up
that a social work professor's deep voice
from long ago reminded me—"It is indeed
more blessed to give than to receive."

Think carefully before you give.

Cataract

Guilt is the letter I owe an ill
poet-friend who wrote me wanting comfort

the heaviness I feel, thinking of tattered linen
face towels waiting for me to feel like ironing

my inability to toss three questionnaires
imploring me to take only a few minutes

my failure to get a committee off its collective
butt in planning a Saturday Night Drop-In

the way I've diddled over summer workshop plans
to take me out of my comfortable rut.

A heavy fog comes down out of nowhere
envelopes me and settles in.

When my eyes needed cataract surgery
my surgeon removed the lens, implanted new lenses.

Guilt is a cataract of the spirit—
covers yellows, blues, greens with indecisive grey.

John on His One Hundred and First Birthday

All of us treat
you as if you were made of fine china

and it is up to us
to wrap you in our caring and solicitude.

You want none of that—
prefer sturdy independence, your cane for years.

You appear each morning
for breakfast, immaculate, ready for the day

walk to the bank, give yourself a haircut
join us for dinner in white starched shirt

tie matching the blue twinkle in your eyes.
Only your tongue occasionally proves traitor.

Taking Hands Crossing the Street

What safer way for two older persons
to get acquainted—a rambling walk.
New building going up.
"Look! Two men way out on that beam."
"No—one's a woman!"

A pleasure, your hand—
big, resolute, only a little shaky
reaching out, mine responding
seeing each other safely across.

Hunger for another human makes
hunger for merely food a paltry thing.
We smile and laugh, feel good today.
Yin and yang walking side by side.
Just in time I remember to ask about your wife.

When I Was Your Age

An Intergenerational Poem

still young enough to marvel
at the infinity of stars
and the neat way humans
are fashioned and expected
to live cozily together,
and someone wished me a Happy New Year!
I sometimes thought—but did not
say, for fear of being thought rude—
I wonder why only one year ahead?
Why not wish me a Happy Life?

And now that I am my age
still marveling at the stars and
the sad way we humans often fail
to make the very most of our humanness
and a friend wishes me a Happy New Year!
he seems to be wishing me an infinity
of days. A whole year ahead!
Three hundred and sixty-five
wonderful star-filled days!
I think—but don't say
for fear of scaring away
any of those days—
how can I be sure I'll live
to get my full quota?
And then I realize all over again
it's not how many but *how*
I use whatever number.

Something you may not yet
have discovered—at your
still-so-tender age.

In Pursuit of a Natural Death

Years ago, when I was still a young thing
we were taking a ride along a winding
road. The road seemed determined to lead us
nowhere, so we almost passed
a pleasant looking, well-fed older mare.
She was dapple grey, mane and tail
still shining. But what made me call STOP!
was that the horse was smiling at me.

"There I am!" I told my still young husband.
"Please stop!" for he was a patient/impatient man
who had just about had it with this road.
Not his idea of a way to spend a sunny afternoon.
He stopped. And I went up to my horse, who
whinnied joyfully, smiled more broadly
clearly not used to all this attention. She let me
pat her, nuzzle my cheek against hers. It was love
between us, that was clear. I could feel
my husband's mental foot tapping. Reluctantly,
we parted. I have never forgotten that horse.

She is with me still, as I think of what a peaceful
natural death she must have had, long since.
Probably just laid down sometime, feeling a little
tired from a rare quasi-gallop. Or maybe she simply
did not wake some morning. She gave me a fine idea.

So now, all these years later
everything is in readiness.
My good doctor agrees—I seem

to be winding down. "The important
thing is to be at peace with yourself."
My body grows weaker, less able. My mind
retains much of its old whimsicality
even a kind of lucidity, which makes it easier
and also harder to free myself to leave.
Two things make me cling until Christmas.
My lovely new book is due out by year's end.
And both my sons plan to spend a few days with me.
Each will give me leave to go. Important.
Should I hang around, my life could
only turn tough. My hope is to leave
while life is still so juicy and tender.

Yet staying or leaving is not up to me.
Whatever comes, I hope it may be a simple
and a natural death. Indeed, isn't that what
we all hope for? Just not waking some morning?

Lost

Total darkness.
No light anywhere.
Wandering. No. Too formal
a term for so lost a feeling.
A kind of nudging along a sort of path
nothing to indicate where.
Was that a sharp
drop-off on one side? Brushing against
weeds or undergrowth on the other.

Finally   a string of lights
like little pricks of pain
or joy or both   indistinguishable
and disappearing almost as soon
as they appeared. The way back.
No way back. Where? *Way back.*
Groping through this dark night
for a lost key. Not-ready feeling.
Suddenly   an opening   to what?

Sensations like lava flow burst
me open. Me. I. Was this
the meaning of this searching?
I am not there. No consciousness.
Now the weeds   the straggly path
even the pinprick lights suddenly
gone   replaced by sensation
wild ecstasy of feeling
as consciousness and I returned.

My Son Dan

is a sociologist. He sits in front
of his word processor or his fax machine
for hours, evaluating data
on health or mental health, comes up
with reports that tell agencies
what they're doing right—and wrong.

When Dan wants me to go to a nutritionist
or a specialist in hurting guts,
he'll say, "Well, it's your choice,
I know, but if I had a gut that hurt
that's what *I'd* do." I can take it
or leave it, which I often do for a spell.
Eventually, I usually see the light.

Tonight, we share some ancient gut screams.
I feel mine quiet down and drift away.

Two grown sons—like but unlike.
Each is as lovable,
loved and loving as is his brother.

Wise Counsel

My son David the psychologist
has a neat way of giving
me excellent advice

while making it seem we are simply
continuing our telephone talk.
This time, he wrote a letter

something not all people still
remember how to do. I had told him
I planned to drop my writers's groups

one at a time, like taking off
a sweater, then shirt and shoes
until I no longer needed any when I

got to the bare state in which all of us
are born. "It sounds to me as if you're
withdrawing just to save the members

discomfort when you die—but if you did
that with all of them, you'd soon die
of boredom. I hope you will take

care of living and let
dying take care of itself."
Splendid advice which I plan to follow!

Back in the Old Days

(an exercise in future-imagining)

When I was still working
even when I still volunteered
a lot during retirement

I used to make lists
to help me keep my life in some semblance
of order   so I wouldn't

turn up at Robertson Day Center
when I was supposed to be at a meeting.
Now I'm limited to one room

and a walk down the hall,
making an occasional grab
for the rail, is a big adventure

meetings are rare as steak
and nobody has asked me to volunteer
for a long time   I still keep lists

try to highlight each day with one
Important Event: Writers' and Poets' Group
Mondays at 1:30 in the library.

Shop at mini-store downstairs.
Phone Dr. B. for appointment.
I decorate with stars   so I won't forget.

To keep my appointment calendar
from looking too spare and bleak   I add
a few elegant   almost illegible scribbles

pleas for funds to answer   bills to pay
anything that covers up the truth
which is that I am slowing down.

Of course any visit from a friend is decorated.
Maybe marked in red. Telephone calls
from my sons are looped about with purple.

Leaning into My Unconscious

I was about to learn
a hidden truth
a gem   flashing
in colored lights   sapphire
white and carmine
the essence, really,
of myself
when an excruciating bolt of pain
struck my left leg
blotting out everything
except   how can I survive
the next few moments?

By the time I'd bent
my knee up close
to my body   held it there
until the pain subsided

nothing was left of my discovery
absolutely zilch   except
the title, which left me
precisely where I'd been
before my flashing of insight—
leaning into my unconscious.
Damn!
Foiled
yet another time

by an overly protective
censor   fearful my fragile psyche
could not bear to learn *The Truth.*

And as I retrieve even this tiny
fragment   tap these few pathetic words
into my word processor   outside my window
a pigeon coos   Who WHo WHO?   WHO YOU   WHO
YOU?

A Straight-On Poem for Ed

Dissembling comes easily
to most of us, call it words
that cover meaning, floating thin as air.

Not to Ed. Somewhere
along his way he lost the art of evasion.
"I like that poem," he'll say.

"In fact, I love that poem.
All except..." and out
he'll come with what's wrong with it.

We've learned to respect his intuitings.

Same way with his feelings.
He listens intently as we wrangle.
"I feel uncomfortable," or, "I sense hostility."

When Ed first came, he made most of *us*
uncomfortable. "I'm a recovering
schizophrenic," he'd say. "I bet you're

scared to have me around?"
And when he said that, we were, a little.
He doesn't say that anymore. No need.

Ed knows he's our barometer. And friend.

Secrets Someone My Age
Should Know the Answers To

This is going to be one of those abominable
"I'm older than you are so listen to me"
poems. It has that smell and sheen.

The way we creep along, like snails, leaving
an iridescent trail of mistakes behind us.

First thing, of course, is to *listen* to our bodies.
The body knows. If blowing smoke rings
eating prime ribs, one high or another begins

to cause us more pain than joy, let it go.
Find another painless joy as substitute.

When your house feels like a burden, why carry it?
Find another small, undemanding home. *Expect*
to move down as your needs slow to a trickle.

Don't let yourself depend wholly on anyone.
All of us depart, some before our lovers are ready.

Why spend a lifetime worrying about something ahead?
Choose to give up driving. Don't wait until
your license is taken away by a judge. Wait too long

and riding light rail and buses will be beyond you.
Listen to yourself. You'll know the answers.

Loving, not being loved, is the best secret I know. *Stop*
mewling about how the one you love fails to meet your needs.
If this irks you, find another lover...if you can.

My Tiny Rumble

So...your instructions are clear?
On who knows what future date, you who are still alive
will open this envelope (and not before!)
place your better ear to the earth
listen for an entire minute—
and say clearly what you hear.
Is the earth rumbling along smoothly
as I heard it this morning?
No complaining, groans, failures
of gears to mesh?
Smooth as fresh mushroom soup
as it slips down your hungry throat?
Well, it's as I expected then.
After all, if I could not detect
any unevenness—with all those trillions
gone before me, their tiny rumbles
ceased—why would it be different when I am no more?
Yes, I confess to a slight disappointment.
Also a relief. For now I know.

Carrying Out the Decision

(for my sister, Ruth)

By the time she gave up,
insisted she no longer wanted
to live, cried out her right to die,
she had dwindled to nearly nothing—
white, frail, hurting, yes, and elderly.
Intravenous needles were removed
after careful consultation
between doctor and family.

And then began
the struggle
between her intermittent feeble wish
and increasing determination
to make an end of it,
between her family's flickering hope
damped by blank fatigue
and belief she never could recover,

between days her doctor seemed
to avoid her door and times
when he was attentive and caring,

and most of all, between a procession
of R.N.s, L.V.N.s, and Nurses' Aides
each trained to sustain life,
confused, resentful, or understanding
when diminished life was rejected.
One crowed over a few sips
of chocolate milk shake,
the next, accepting death,
noted without expression
Intake: 0.

A Joyous Way

Along with most of you
death is not what I fear
for why fear what I may not know?

My knotted gut this early morning
reminds me of another fear, far
sharper than death for me:

any lingering illness
especially if both eye and I
have fled my sadly shrunken self.

There yet remains a third bogey.
What if I lack the sense to let go,
insist on striving long past my time?

To briefly have
but not to hold
ah! there's a joyous way to go.

Pre-Visualization

In photography, good seeing
and pre-visualization are all,
my teacher taught me.

In poetry, better to meander—
at least at first
find meaning
from one brilliant flash
ripping apart the dark underside
of the moon
not worry if it sometimes takes years
for the flash to appear.

If I could pre-visualize how—and when—
my large, loose expanse of skin
this plethora of faltering
formerly interlinking highways
my only intermittently
sparking brain
and conflicted feelings
would simultaneously decide
to give up this life,
if I *could* know in advance
I'm not sure I'd want that.
Would you?

Saying Good-Bye

My mother was never one for good-byes
not even the ordinary ones. That night
when we both knew what we should have said
she just turned her head when I left,
acted as if she hadn't heard me say
"I'll see you in the morning."
Cowards. We both knew I might come
but she would be gone.

She didn't want to bid her own mother
good-bye either, and refused to let
me or my older sister go into the room
to give our grandma one last kiss
when Grandma, all propped up
in her four-poster, lay gasping for breath.
"Some things people have to do alone,"
my mother said, her mouth in a straight line.

But Grandma and I understood each other.
When I brought her breakfast tray
I'd hear her tiny voice murmuring
"Swing low, sweet cha-ri-o-o-t,
comin' for to carry me home,"
so I knew she knew
and was ready, long past ready.
I stroked her thin silvery hair,
washed her soft wrinkled face
and together we'd sing
"Sweet cha-ri-o-o-t..."

There are worse ways to take one's leave.

Quicksilver

First, a red line
flowing from my left nostril.
A moving line   but barely.
The blood was deep red, I noted
as if it were happening to someone else.

I stanched the flow with a Kleenex,
two, three. I remember tossing
them into my wastebasket
and thinking those who found me
would know I'd been warned.

Nothing else happened.
I finished brushing my teeth, flossed
as usual, smoothed on my nightly aloe
and lanolin, turned off the former
Secretaries of State, still discussing

how we got into the muddle we're in
and went to bed. The last I remember
thinking was that my nosebleed was like
what happened to first my mother, then
my husband, but only in color—both of them

had died with massive hemorrhages.
I puttered around a few minutes in case
something else happened. Nothing did.
I was almost asleep when suddenly my body
felt as if quicksilver were being drawn up

and I was poised for flight. So this is it,
I thought. Could it be I would be so blessed   to go
with only a gathering-up sensation   no pain?
As I wondered, a second quicksilver attack.
This one stronger than the first, but now I felt

resistance to the drawing, a definite pulling back.
Whatever was happening to me seemed totally
apart from my volition. I had a moment
of thinking of my two sons, their families
as if to salute them as I passed by. Then slowly

I found myself still alive, not bleeding, no
more quicksilver, nothing. Only a feeling
of being blessed beyond what I deserved.
I thought of all those I loved, gone before,
and hoped they, too, had felt the quicksilver.

Please Remember

says the gold-framed sign,
inconspicuous—only five by eight—
except to those of us who know to look.

Bare bones only. So and so
passed away on such and such. Apartment number.
Perhaps he or she had lived among us

twelve or thirteen years, was ready
to give up this known for an unknown. Or
someone who'd moved in eight days before

heartsick at losing first her husband
then the home they'd shared for thirteen years,
too distraught to listen to counsels of "Wait!"

No mention of family. If we had known
the late so and so (late for what? I wonder)
we might know she had a caring daughter

or that no relative ever came to visit,
a little-by-little death. No hint of how this death
occurred, not even, maybe especially, that

as happened once in my nearly a year here
she had thrown herself out her eleventh floor
window, an end apartment viewing on the capitol.

I cannot bear to think only my bones
will be listed. So here's what I would like—
a kind of good-bye in case I don't have time for more.

Janet Carncross Chandler (all three names, please)
wife of Bill for fifty-two years, until his death in 1984
mother of two loving sons and their families—

David and Beverly, son William; Dan and Betty, daughter Sasha.
After thirty years as social worker, Janet became—
somewhat to her surprise—a poet after retirement,

with six published books of poetry about relationships.
She died after a (brief or long) illness while dancing
about her apartment, quite alone.

Janet said to tell you there are many of you
she cared about, especially the writers. She played
an erratic game of pool and did a lot of volunteering.

Requiem

Here lies the body of a poem
close as my breath   distant as a star
brightly beckoning for only one brief moment
then gone forever   never to return again
greatly missed by all the millions
who would have known and loved her
especially her mourning mother

About the Author

Janet Carncross Chandler, eighty-three, lives in a Sacramento retirement community. She is the mother of two, David and Dan, and the grandmother of two, William and Sasha. She was a social worker for thirty years prior to her retirement in 1971. She holds an M.F.A. in Writing from Goddard College (1988) and an M.S.W. from the George Warren Brown School of Social Work, Washington University in St. Louis (1960). Now a poet for nineteen years, she has self-published three chap-books—*The Colors of a Marriage* (1982), *Poems for Poets and Other Fragile Humans* (1983), and *"How Are You" They Ask New Widow* (1985)—as well as *Significant Relationships* (1988), and published *Flight of the Wild Goose* (Papier-Mache Press, 1989). Her poetry has appeared in numerous poetry journals, and she has authored three plays.

Ms. Chandler has participated in numerous writers and poets groups, both as a member and as a facilitator. She is still active in the Pioneer Tower Writers and Poets, which she started in 1989. She has also taken an interest in several senior organizations, including membership in the Older American's Month Planning Commission for the Sacramento County Commission on Aging, the Unitarian Universalist Society of Sacramento, and the Older Women's League.

Quality Books from Papier-Mache Press

At Papier-Mache Press our goal is to produce attractive, accessible books that deal with contemporary personal, social, and political issues. Our titles have found an enthusiastic audience in general interest, women's, new age, and Christian bookstores, as well as in gift stores, mail order catalogs, and libraries. Many have also been used by teachers for women's studies, creative writing, and gerontology classes, and by therapists and family counselors to help clients explore personal issues such as aging and relationships.

If you are interested in finding out more about our titles, ask your local bookstores which Papier-Mache items they carry. Or, if you would like to receive a complete catalog of books, posters, and shirts from Papier-Mache Press, please send a self-addressed stamped envelope to:

Papier-Mache Press
135 Aviation Way, #14
Watsonville, CA 95076